Guide to the Hidden Land of
the Yolmo Snow Enclosure and its History

Guide to the
HIDDEN LAND of the
YOLMO
SNOW ENCLOSURE
and its HISTORY

Khenpo Nyima Dondrup

Vajra Publications
www.vajrabooks.com.np

Published by

Vajra Publications
Jyatha, Thamel, Kathmandu, Nepal
Tel.: 977-1-4220562, Fax: 977-1-4246536
e-mail: bidur_la@mos.com.np
www.vajrabooks.com.np; www.vajrabookshop.com

Distributed by

Vajra Book Shop
Kathmandu, Nepal

Author's contact address

79 Sundar Marg, Boudha-6
Kathmandu, Nepal
Phone: 4499838
khennyima@hotmail.com

ISBN No. 978-9937-506-46-5

Printed in Nepal

Guide to the Hidden Land of the Yolmo Snow Enclosure and its History

Khenpo Nyima Dondrup

The lord Buddha, completely accomplished in the two accumulations
The sublime Dharma, authoritative in scriptural learning and experiential realisation
The noble Sangha, with the dual endowment of intelligence and transcendence
These are the three rare and precious objects of salutation

To the north of the land of Nepal, birthplace of the lord Buddha Sakyamuni, on the Himalayan borders of Nepal and Tibet, is the hidden land of Yolmo, enclosure of snows, also known as Padma Tsal, 'lotus grove sanctuary'. Concerning the prophecy of this hidden land in the Avatamsaka Sutra, it is written in the 'Hundred thousand songs of Milarepa' that Marpa told Mila 'The Riwo Pelbar mountain in Mangyul and the Yolmo snow enclosure in Nepal are places prophesied in the Avatamsaka Sutra, so meditate there!' It is a place visited and blessed by Guru Rinpoché of Odiyana and his consorts. They filled the mountains and valleys with religious and material treasures, and described in the 'Guide to Padma Tsal' and future prophecies, the 'Crucial guide to the Yolmo snow enclosure', the 'Essential inventory of Yolmo', the 'Crucial inventory of the Yolmo snow enclosure', the 'Essential exposition' inventory of prophecies for the Yolmo snow

1

enclosure, the 'Name inventory of the hidden lands' and so forth, are the layout of this valley, the prescription for identifying the suitable time to discover it, the identification of the discoverer, the means for taking possession of it, and the benefits of going there and remaining there, as delivered to the Tibetan Dharmaraja Trisong Détsen and then concealed as treasure. These were revealed by Tértön Rikdzin Chenpo Göki Demtru Chen (1337-1408). As directed by Marpa, Jétsun Milarepa (1041-1123) spent three years in the Lion fort tiger cave in Yolmo, planted the banner of spiritual attainment, and perfected his realisation.

When the time eventually came for the fulfillment of the prophecies by lord Buddha and Padmasambhava of Odiyana, the transmissions of the precious Sutra and Mantra teachings that flourished in this hidden land for centuries were principally the 'Changtér' ('northern revelations') of Rikdzin Gödem and the 'rainbow' transmission from the profound revelations of Orgyen Létro Lingpa (1585-1656), these two.

Nyingma Tradition

First, concerning the spread of the Nyingma teachings, chiefly the Changtér, it seems that Gödem's disciple Drupchen Palden Gyeltsen founded a temple at Yangri Gang, as foreseen in the Guru's list of prophecies. In the 'Chariot of certainty' biography of Rikdzin Surya Sengé, it is said that Druptop Gyeltsen Bum had earlier founded a temple at Yangri in fulfillment of the prophecy, and there is an oral tradition to that effect, but Gyeltsen Bum's biography confirms the founder as Gödem's disciple Palden Gyeltsen, and states that Gyeltsen Bum restored it and resided there. This means that the first Nyingmapa temple was founded there in the 14th century, yet it is widely claimed that the great Tértön and Vidyadhara Ngakchang Shakya Sangpo opened the hidden valley of Yolmo, founded the temple called 'Tsuti', or 'Dzoedril', as his residence there, and established the teaching of the Sutra and Mantra teachings in general, and the Changtér teachings in particular, which are likened to the minister of Tibet (because they emphasise protection and so forth). The biographical account of previous births says of Shakya Sangpo 'He also opened the great hidden valley of Yolmo, enclosure of snows', and the 'History of the

Nyingma tradition' states that 'He opened the gate to the Yolmo valley and revealed the instructions on 'Mahakarunika, liberator of Samsara into the expanse of space.' According to the 'Variegated jewel garland' Nepal itinerary by the 6th Shamarpa Chöki Wangchuk (1584-1630), 'This Dzoedril Gönpa, so-named because of the triangular stone Torma which verified the site during Ngakchang Shakya Sangpo's prognosis at Riwo Pelbar in Mangyul, or because it is the place 'where the ox (Dzo) fell over (Dril)', was the seat of the Ngakchang, his reincarnation Namka Gyachin and so on, up to the present Yolmo Tulku Tendzin Norbu....'

Concerning this noble master's thorough restoration of the Charung Kashor Stupa (Boudhanath) in accord with prophecy, the biographical account of previous births says 'Unhesitatingly, he proceeded to Nepal. At that time, the Charung Kashor Stupa had become a hill indistinguishable from others, and at first he prostrated before another hill thinking it was the one, which turned to dust, and this hill was next to the Stupa. When he then located it for sure, and started a major renovation, there was no water in the vicinity, and saying that "There must be water here", he listened (to the earth), and heard the trickling sound 'Trol-trol', and dug in that place, and water flowed out, and still flows to this day. It was most extraordinary, and the recollection of having been born as a supplicant of Buddha Kasyapa's teachings long ago occurred to him.'

Later on, it was written in the biography of Situ Rinpoché Chöki Jungné (1700-76), as quoted in the 'History of the Dharma delightful to the wise, entitled Music of marvellous tales', that '[The Stupa] that we still call Charung Kashor is known to the Newars themselves as "Kawa Chaitya". "Kawa" seems to be a derivation of "Kata", thus meaning "excavated Stupa", which could indicate Yolmowa Shakya Sangpo's excavation of an earth mound to reveal the buried Stupa', so the story that the Stupa had become buried over time due to neglect or whatever reason, and through the fruition of his aspiration this great treasure revealer was able to restore it as a field for the accumulation of merit, seems to have some foundation, be that as it may.

Since Shakya Sangpo was a teacher of Ngari Panchen Pema Wangyé (1487-1542) and his younger brother Lekden Düjom Dorjé, this would seem to place his opening of the Yolmo valley and foundation of the Tsuti monastery in the early 16th century. His reincarnation

Namka Gyachin is said in the Guide by Shamar Chöki Wangchuk quoted above to have spent time in Yolmo, but no detailed biography has become available. The autobiography of the 3rd Yolmo Tulku Tendzin Norbu (1598-1644) mentions that he established the temple of the caretakers of the Charung Kashor Stupa, now known as Guru Lhakhang, that he revealed a hidden spring nearby, and that he visited and meditated in Yolmo, where his predecessors were based. From the statement in the 'outer' biography of Zilnön Wangyé Dorjé that during the tenure of his descendant (Wönpo) Namka Pelsang, obstacles caused the Tsuti Gönpa to burn down and it was duly restored, we learn that Shakya Sangpo's family lineage remained in Yolmo.

Tendzin Norbu appointed his disciple Rikdzin Yolmowa Topden Wangpo Chimé Gyatso, an incarnation whose emanational source was Vajrapani and whose previous births included Lhalung Pelki Dorjé, in charge of nine temples in Yolmo and Nepal, chiefly the estate of the great Charung Kashor Stupa. There was a temple founded either by this Lama or one of his predecessors in the area above the cemetery at Melamchi, as recounted in the oral tradition of the local elders, and Tendzin Norbu's biography records that while in Yolmo he visited Tsuti Gönpa, the Yangdak Chok cave and Melamchi. At the time Zilnön Wangyé Dorjé visited Lhasa at the age of 13 to take ordination from the 5th Dalai Lama, his father Topden Wangpo Chimé Gyatso passed away at the Orgyen Ling Gönpa, and when passing through the Kathmandu valley on his return, king Pratap Malla told him "It is sad that your father the Kashor Lama did not remain longer with us, but as the saying 'goes, the son takes the place of his deceased father, and the gums take the place of lost teeth, so you must do your best. Moreover, as you have brought blessings on this land in all your previous lives, the custodianship of the Yolmo temples, Melamchi, Kyéwalung and so on, and most of all the great Kashor Stupa, must not change", as is recounted in his 'outer' biography. This shows that there was a temple at Melamchi before Zilnön Wangyé Dorjé founded an Amitabha chapel there.

Concerning the presence to this day of a family lineage of Lhalung Pelki Dorjé in Yolmo and the region: following the prophecy of Tendzin Norbu, and prophecies by the raven-faced Mahakala, Dorjé Lekpa and so on, Topden Wangpo Chimé Gyatso married the daughter of Bhisanga Pel, the local ruler of Temal. Their son was Zilnön Wangyé

4

Dorjé, and his two sons Tsédak Dorjé and Gyaltsap Dorjé lived in Yolmo, and it is from them that this lineage descended. In later life, Zilnön Wangyé Dorjé lived in Gangtar Chung and so on, and a family lineage continued there too, who must also have been the family descendants of Topden Wangpo Chimé Gyatso.

Following the prophecy in the 'Crucial guide to the Yolmo snow enclosure' that 'To the west is a mountain like a queen with flowing robe/ Below it, an Amitabha chapel and a great centre for the pursuit of virtue should be established', the 4th Yolmo Tulku Zilnön Wangyé Dorjé (1647-1716) founded such a chapel at Melamchi in the 7th or 8th decade of the 17th century. The 'outer' biography, which he dictated, says 'Mahacharya Padmasambhava declared that to protect sentient beings in the age of the five degenerations, a great temple should be founded on the western mountain resembling a queen with flowing robe in the great hidden land of Yolmo, enclosure of snows, and I did so accordingly. Thinking that some beings might want to live there, I stayed for 17 years, but in that time, apart from myself and my disciples, not a single person came there, so that it has not served to inculcate merit in the beings of the present, who are disinclined to hardship. May the great emanation of Odiyana have mercy!'

Thus, a temple was built, a clay statue of Buddha Amitabha was installed as the main image, and the Guru's jewel millstone and so on was also there. The 'Guide to Padma Tsal' says 'There is the jewel millstone', and Tendzin Norbu's biography records that during his visit to Melamchi, he showed that the Guru's jewel millstone was not turning spontaneously (as people thought),) but made it shake, as witnessed by all present, and this was one of the great blessings of the Yolmo valley. This seat of the Changtér teachings and community for the exposition and practice of the teachings continued under the tutelage of the sons, Tsédak Dorjé and Gyaltsap Dorjé, the disciple Nyima Sengé, and so forth.

Zilnön Wangyé Dorjé's disciple Rikdzin Surya (Nyima) Sengé (1687-1738), of the family lineage of Orgyen Tennyi Lingpa, put an end to an epidemic in the Kathmandu valley in about 1723, and seeing him as a Buddha incarnate, the king's court presented him with local costume, turban, two thousand silver coins worth of rice growing land and a copper plate certificate for as long as his teaching lineage continued. The edict was despatched with representatives, but the Lama summoned all the local elders to a feast, and announced that he wanted land. Accordingly, he was offered all the land from Langra Gyalsa to Drupa Drong for as long as his teaching lineage endured, and he established a religious estate and residence at Langra Gyalsa called Sang-ngak Déchen Ling. In 1725, in accord with the Yolmo prophecies, he founded a temple on the top of Yangri mountain, the heart of the sanctuary, which is like a precious Stupa, but after only three years it was reduced to ashes in an elemental Mandala (ie; a fire). In the Earth Bird year 1729 he founded another temple in Langra Gyalsa, known as the Padma Chöling retreat centre. He also had a Mani prayer wheel erected in the village and so on. He instituted many religious observances, such as performing the Mandala-s of the three heart Sadhana-s (outer, inner and secret) on the tenth day of the month, and an annual week-long Drupchö or ritual performance of the Narak Dongtruk Sadhana ('churning the depths of hell'). There were many who came to do three year retreats, engage in the Vajrayana practices, meditate on the 'sunlight' instructions of the Great Perfection, stay in dark retreat and so on. As it is said,

'With the three gates constantly engaged in Dharma/ Planting the banner of spiritual attainment in solitary havens/ May my aspiration for the early translation teachings of Vajrayana be fulfilled!'

Surya Sengé's son and successor was Rikdzin Trinlé Düjom (1726-89), also known as Rikdzin Gönangpa Chenpo. With the greater or lesser contributions of his monks and disciples, he established one of the largest Mani prayer wheels in the Yolmo valley, apparently the one that is still there, near the cemetery. In 1749-50, he again restored the temple, or 'great support of worship that liberates on sight', on Yangri Gang, but it was destroyed by lightning. So it was that first Gödem's disciple Palden Gyeltsen, then Druptop Gyeltsen Bum, Surya Sengé and Trinlé Düjom built temples there in accord with the prophecy, but due to the reduced merit of the beings of the degenerate age, and in particular those in Tibet, they were all destroyed by lightning. Further, he commissioned storey-tall statues of Mahacharya Padmasamhava, flanked by Mahakarunika and the wrathful Guru (Dorjé Drakpo Tsel), for the assembly hall of the Langra Gyalsa temple, and arrow-height statues of Mahakarunika and Dorjé Drakpo Tsel for the Yangdak Chok hermitage. Thus he commissioned symbols of enlightened body, speech and mind, and engaged in the three spheres of teaching activity, such as giving empowerments, transmissions and instruction, and made it compulsory for the monks and nuns in his community to spend one month a year in retreat, and for lay devotees to perform the Nyungné fast once a month, or at least on holy days.

Thus, since Drupchen Palden Gyeltsen's foundation of a temple on Yangri in the 14th century, the great Tértön Shakya Sangpo and his disciples, the second Yolmo incarnation Namka Gyachin, the third Tendzin Norbu, the throneholder of Tsuti Gönpa Wönpo Namka Pelsang, the senior disciple of Tendzin Norbu Rikdzin Yolmowa Topden Wangpo Chimé Gyatso, his son the fourth Yolmo incarnation Zilnön Wangyé Dorjé, his sons Tsédak Dorjé and Gyaltsap Dorjé, senior disciple Térwön Nyima Sengé, his sons Rikdzin Trinlé Düjom and Tendzin Gyurmé Dorjé, his son Chimé Orgyen Tendzin and the latter's younger brother Tséwang Sonam Gyatso and so on founded and restored temples in the hidden land of Yolmo, and spread the teachings of the Sutra and Mantrayana in general, and in particular the precious transmitted, revealed and visionary teachings of the Changtér tradition, chiefly the revelations of Rikdzin Gödemchen. The first temple of the Changtér tradition in this hidden land was at Yangri Gang, the second was Tsuti Gönpa, the third was the Amitabha chapel at Melamchi, and fourth was the Padma Chöling hermitage monastery at Langra Gyalsa, as already related, and gradually other monasteries produced by these teaching and family lineages grew up in Yolmo and other places.

Kagyu Tradition

In the 'Hundred thousand songs of Milarepa', it is written:

'I bow to the noble Lama/ Whom I encountered due to my accumulated merit/
Now I have reached the place of attainment indicated by him/
Pleasant stronghold in the forested mountains of Mön/
Land of flower-spangled meadows/
Forest clearing where the trees dance (ie; sway in the wind)/
Where the monkeys play/ Where all kinds of birdsong is heard/
Where bees hover/ Where rainbows shimmer day and night/
In such a secluded place/ I , the Yogi Milarepa/

Experience the blissful luminosity of meditation on mind as void'

And also:

'Within the sanctuary of Sengéla/ Milarepa meditates on emptiness/ There is no fear of meditation going astray/ Only the courage of long persistence'

And:

'Being in such a place is naturally pleasant/ Without a single companion, even more so'

Milarepa's Takpuk Sengé Dzong meditation cave, referred to in these songs, is in this hidden land.

Shamar Chöki Wangchuk's 'Variegated jewel garland' Nepal itinerary records:

'We arrived at Götsang Ling, where Götsang Réchen, the disciple of Tsangnyön Heruka (1452-1507), stayed and founded the first monastic hermitage....'

The founder of Götsang Ling was Götsang Réchen Natsok Rangdröl (1482-1559), and in his 'Ocean of Siddhi-s' verse autobiography, it says:

'On the tenth day of the eleventh month of the Tiger year/ At dawn came good portents and a feeling of warmth...' and it also says '....as well as at Chuwar, the 'six forts', and in Yolmo....', so I assume he was there in the early 16th century. According to the itinerary just cited, he established the first monastic hermitage, as well as a religious estate (Labrang), but it seems that the temple was built later. In the 'Wish fulfilling jewel, source of all things desirable, radiating fabulous light' biography of his disciple Khédrup Chenpo Jampa Puntsok (1503-81), we read:

'In the autumn of the Dragon year (1556) when I was 54, while travelling in Nepal, I passed through Langtang down to Yolmo, where my hosts requested the Saroruha initiation and so on, and tendered excellent hospitality, establishing a pure connection. When I reached Götsang Ling in Yolmo, I recalled my old Lama, thinking how much he had done to benefit others in his time there, and shed many tears. Repeatedly recalling Chojé Götsangpa in this melancholic mood, I saw him in a dream looking absolutely splendid, wearing the eight garments of the cemetery. After singing many songs of realisation, he declared:

"A mind free of deceit has the Pratimoksa commitment/
A mind continually preoccupied with benefitting others has the Bodhicitta commitment/
Purification of grasping at the ordinary characteristics of phenomena is the Tantric vow/
All else is meaningless, OM AH HUM!"

At that time, I began a course of instruction in the four syllables and six Yoga-s at Götsang Ling which went on for a month and a half. In that period, at the Götsang Ling Labrang, I recalled the master's life again and again, and his introduction to the profound nature dominated my thoughts. At that time, Lama Kunga had died before the completion of the temple and copying of the extended Prajnaparamita scripture, so his successors, the disciples and sponsors called on me to perform consecration, and we had an extensive ceremony. The Yolmo people arranged the puja and offerings to perfection, as is their custom.'

Thus the temple was built by Lama Kunga and consecrated by Jampa Puntsok in 1556.

Later on, Karma Chösang from Réchung Puk, disciple of the reincarnation of Götsang Repa Karma Drupchok Wangpo (1563-1618), came to Yolmo, as is well known to the followers of the 'Rainbow' teachings there. This must have been in the early years of the 17th century, since Drupchok Wangpo took the throne of Réchung Puk in later life, according to the 'Moon crystal garland' history of Buddhism by Situ Chöki Jungné. Initially the practice tradition there was Kagyupa, but later holders of the teaching and family lineages favoured the 'rainbow' teachings (Jatsön Chökor) revealed by Rikdzin Jatsön Nyingpo, and the Kagyupa tradition was no longer evident.

The first propagator of the Jatsön teachings in border regions like Yolmo was Ngoktön Karma Losang. His dates are not known, but he was educated in the Nyingma tradition, and went on to study with many teachers, chiefly Drupchok Wangpo for seven years, and the 6th Shamar Chöki Wangchuk, and became a master of the teachings unconfined by any school. Concerning his coming to Yolmo, his autobiography records:

9

'Coming from Nyanang along the valley route, I was carried from one place to the next always by chair. In a succession of welcoming and farewell gatherings, I gave a constant round of empowerments to those I met along the way, in the name of benefitting living beings, while coins fell like rain. Thus, performing so many Torma ceremonies, fire pujas and tenth day offerings, I reached Yolmo without my feet touching the ground. I was thinking of holding a three month winter teaching session, but due to an invitation by (some other) sponsors, I held classes for just over a month. I gave the thirty or so young monks who attended 100 coins and sent them off to Réchung Puk (in central Tibet). I had the Götsang Ling temple restored, bringing wood and summoning craftsmen to put up a new roof. Following the Lama's last wishes and with the consent of his five sons, their wives and the two grandmothers, I gave whatever support was necessary. The family lineage holders (Wönpo) were each one keener than the next, and in particular the senior Wönpo, Karma Guru Rinpoché, a powerful Mantrika with a reputation for accomplishment, became my disciple. In my dream, on the night before I was to meet the reincarnation of his Lama, I encountered (his) father Tokden Gyalpo Jampa Namgyal, who said "There is the reincarnation of the head (or deceased?) Lama, you should recognise him."'

And later, when making the commitment of complete renunciation at Drakar:

'Also at that time, when the two brothers Lama Guru and Kagyu were at Yolmo Götsang Ling, I gave a hundred coins for the restoration of the temple, and a hundred coins and 3 Sho of gold were given for starting a programme of meditation on Guru Padmasambhava at the Yangdak Chok hermitage. This was a way of introducing the 'Union of the rare and supreme' (Könchok Chidü) practice. Then the Kyédün Drupchen was instituted there. I offered 130 coins, and 100 coins to those practising the new teachings....The two Mantrika Guru-s were enthroned at Götsang Ling and Orgyen Ling.'

Thus, at the time of Ngoktön Karma Losang's visit to Yolmo, five brothers, chiefly Karma Guru and Kagyu, were resident at Götsang Ling, and since Karma Losang's establishment of the Jatsön teaching cycle in the 17th century, their descendants and other practitioners of the Jatsön teachings founded many more monasteries across the region. Later on, teachers such as Rikdzin Tséwang Norbu, Rikdzin Trinlé Düjom and Drakarwa Chöki Wangchuk expounded the Changtér and Jatsön teachings extensively, and composed many writings as well. So for centuries, the most renowned teachings in the Yolmo valley were the Changtér revelations of Rikdzin Gödemchen and the 'Jatsön Poedruk' ('six rainbow volumes') revelations of Rikdzin Jatsön Nyingpo.

Later on, from about 1981, Chatral Sangyé Dorjé, the regent of Guru Padmasambhava of Odiyana, praised in an undeceiving Vajra prophecy from the 'Future Prophecies' of Yönru Chimé Dorjé as 'Supreme heart emanation of (Guru) Padma/ Son blessed by Vimalamitra/ Born in an ox year, with the name Vajra/ He will advance the teachings of the practice tradition', established retreat centres at Drupé Drong, Néding, Sermatang and Lhakhang, 'opened' the Tongshong meditation cave of Guru Padma, composed a 'Praise of the Yolmo sanctuary' and 'Evocation of the hidden land', and lovingly and impartially conferred profound teachings for the attainment of a body of light in a single lifetime and the empowerments, transmissions and instructions of the Great Perfection on worthy recipients. Thus even at the end of the aeon, the Sutra and Mantra teachings in general, and in particular the precious teachings of the luminous Great Perfection of the early translation tradition of six greatnesses were widespread in the king of hidden valleys, the snow enclosure of Yolmo.

Similarly, Kyapjé Düjom Rinpoché, Kyapjé Drupwang Penor Rinpoché and Kyapjé Doedrup Rinpoché set foot in this hidden valley, and conferred their blessings and teachings with supreme kindness. Following the wishes of Drupwang Penor Rinpoché, Khenchen Pema Sherab Rinpoché spent years giving vast and profound teachings to Lama-s. monks and ordinary folk, and the kindness of these great masters is beyond measure, since 'to uphold the precious teachings of the Buddha through explication and practical accomplishment is the intention of the Buddha-s and Bodhisattva-s.'

The Guidebooks

Now, to enjoin the enthusiasm of the faithful and strengthen belief in the sanctity of the valley, I shall summarise the topography, great qualities and benefits of visiting it, as they appear in the prophetic guidebooks.

The 'Guide to the hidden valley of Padma Tsal' says 'Whether known as the Yolmo snow enclosure/ Or as the 'lotus grove' hidden valley, it is the same/ It's configuration is as follows/ Summit overlooking the meeting of six uplands/ The joining of three valleys/ At the throat of the high snows/ To the north of Vajrasana/ Northeast of the city of Li/ At the foot of the land of Mangyul/ At the throat of the Buddha's own devotee (Gényen Leru)/ At the throat of the western side of the chief of the twelve territorial goddesses (Tséringma)....

The rear mountain is like a child in his mother's lap/ The eastern mountain is like a king on his throne/ The southern mountains are bowed down/ The western mountain is like a raised Vajra with three prongs/ The white rock of the northern mountain is marked with a Svasti design/ The three plateaux are in the form of a lotus flower/ There is the jewel millstone....

In later times, there will be seven thousand tent households in the upper valley and/ Seven thousand settlements in the lower valley/ There the Mantrayana teachings will shine like the rising sun/ Reside there in summer and in Liyul in winter....

The one who discovers this sacred place will be one who has accumulated limitless merit/ One with Karmic destiny, the emanation of myself, Padmasambhava.'

The 'Crucial guide to the Yolmo snow enclosure' says: 'In the valley known as the Yolmo snow enclosure/ Over two Yojana-s east of the Riwo Pelbar mountain/ Is the king of snow mountains, like a victory banner held aloft/ On it's south side/ All the upper mountainsides are snow covered/ Below that, they are as if divided between glacial scree and meadow/ Below that they are beautified by abundant wild forest/ The valley floor is like an eight petalled lotus/ Where nutritious grain and other fruits grow in season/ A land of seven thousand settlements/ There are four secret doors in the four directions/ All who go there will know content/ All who are born there will be freed from the bonds of cyclic existence/ All who hear of it will develop virtuous renunciation/ It is the essential field of my teaching activity, Padmasambhava of Odiyana/ Where the Buddhist teachings will be found in the age of degeneration/ And boundless good qualities....

From the centre of that land, all directions can be seen as if in a mirror/ The centre is like a jewel-filled platter/ The king's abode should be established there/ The hills to the north of that are disposed like a jewel Stupa/ Build a Vidyadhara temple of Padmasambhava at their foot, and/ Establish there a community for the propagation of virtue in this land/ To the east is a fair meadow like a silk drape/ Alongside it, build a temple to Shakya Sengé and/ A domain of the ordained Sangha/ To the south is a mountainside of forest and meadow/ At it's centre, build a temple of Avalokitesvara and/ A domain for all/ To the west is a mountain like a queen with flowing robe/ In front of it. build a temple of Amitabha and/ A great (monastery) for the pursuit of virtue/ In the northern hills resembling a precious Stupa/ Is a cave facing southeast/ That is the sacred place where I, Padmasambhava of Odiyana, performed meditation on Yangdak Chok/ From the peak above, one can see the (Asura) cave at Yangleshö/ Those who go there will be freed from birth in the lower realms/ I declare that those who meditate on devotion to mé, Padmasambhava/ Shall see my face and/ Attain the Siddhi-s of the supreme Mahamudra in this life/ Also, signifying and symbolising that the features and/ Configurations of this land are blessed, there are many precious deposits/ When nearly fifty lifetimes have elapsed, these will be discovered/ Once those with the right Karmic destiny have come there/ Seven thousand settlements will grow up/ And the Mantrayana teachings will be like a flag flying high.'

According to the 'Essential inventory of Yolmo': 'The valley known as the Yolmo snow enclosure/ At the foot of Mangyul/ Northeast of the city of Li/ South of the snow mountain resembling a victory banner/ West of the Yaksi snow queen/ There are three great valleys/ And three minor ones/ From top to bottom it is four days journey/ There are seven great deposits of treasure/ Various medicinal substances occur there/ At the waist of the valley is a medicinal spring/ In the upper valley is a glacial stream of water of the eight qualities/ There are three great lakes/ As there are many Dakini-s and Ksetrapala-s/ One must refrain from the defilements of pollution and conflict/ This is a most auspicious sanctuary/ Where longevity, merits and resources all multiply/ Those living in the degenerate who would practise what I (Padmasambhava) have taught/ Go find that sanctuary!/ Those who think of it and long for it/ Have accumulated merit over limitless aeons/ Bodhisattva-s who proceed there/ Are Bodhisattva-s on the ten stages of the path/ My field of teaching activity during the degenerate age is that sanctuary/ Karmically endowed individuals of the future should strive to find it out!/ Such is my testament/ One born in that place/ Has fortunate destiny/ Has accumulated merit.'

The 'Crucial inventory of the Yolmo snow enclosure' says: 'Seventy adepts accomplished in Mantrayana shall come/ Eleven (who attain liberation) in this body shall come....

West of the Tashi Tséringma snow mountain/ Northeast of the city of Li/ Is the lotus grove hidden land/ A valley in the form of a standing lotus/ From it's upper peaks, the Liyul valley can be seen.'

And in the 'Essential exposition' inventory of prophecies for the Yolmo snow enclosure: 'The three sanctuaries are/ The Yolmo snow enclosure/ Between southern Mangyul and Nyanang/ Rolpa Khandro Ling, between Sin and Bü/ And Drémoshong, between Zar and Lamo/ In these three, all beings beleaguered by suffering must seek liberation....

Looking west from that mountain, there is a mountain like a mother with her son in her lap/ Going before it and looking around from there/ One sees the eastern mountain, like a king on his throne/ All the mountains to the south are bowed down/ The western mountain is like a three-pronged Vajra held aloft/ All the mountains to the north stand in protection....

To the south of the heap-like hill at the heart of the sanctuary/ Is a white cliff marked with Svasti design/ On the side of a white cliff like an offering cake, to the side of the valley/ Is a deposit of precious jewels seven times sealed/ Many different grains grow in the surrounding plateaux and valleys/ A variety of wild animals lives there/ Various medicinal plants grow/ There should be a prohibition on hunting in the upper valleys/ Gateway Stupa-s should be built in the four directions/ There are hidden deposits of the five precious substances/ There is a perfect assembly of good qualities/ In particular, at the head of the valley is a white rock mountain with three separate peaks/ At it's waist/ Digging with a diamond chisel, inside is a gold amulet box, with the capacity of thirteen Samyé volume measures/ Inside is the heart of Acharya Shantigarbha/ Bearing self-arisen images of the Manjuyama deity cycle/ There are seven gold elephants adorned with seven kinds of jewels/ In a silver jar is the left thumb of the Odiyana Dakini

Siddhikara on which an image of Vajravarahi appeared naturally/ Three leather amulet boxes, each with the capacity of three Samyé volume measures/ Are filled with jewels of six kinds brought from an island in the ocean/ There is a hand-sized wooden flask filled with the nectar of immortality offered to Guru Padma by the planetary deity Rahula/ Seven golden bowls the size of a cupped pair of hands/ These things will be revealed much later by an emanation (of Guru Padma)/ To the northwest of the valley is a square red rock/ In the centre of a boulder at it's foot/ Is a silver jar containing a golden measure (Bre) with nine kinds of precious jewels/ On the central mountain like a heap of rice/ To the southwest, is a stone amulet box with fitting lid/ Inside is a dark wooden chest two square metres (Dom) in size/ In there are the Sadhana-s of seven Dakini-s, Great Perfection teachings merely to see which is to attain Buddhahood/ Seven volumes/ Over a hundred scrolls/ Shantigarbha's 61 blade wheel for wrathful Mantra rites/ A hundred jewel letters/ Large enough to accomodate seven visitors/ These will be revealed after seven generations of human settlement in the valley/ Thus there are seven great treasure deposits/ Sixty one minor deposits/ Three instructions/ Seven self-manifest deities/ And seven self-manifest signs/ Making this valley like a jewel island.'

The 'Name inventory of the hidden lands' says: 'The forested lower valleys are narrow but secure/ In these secure minor valleys/ I, Padma, the king of Odiyana/ Have pacified the ground, given blessings and hidden teachings for future revelation/ Appointed vigilant guardian spirits/ Thus the meditation places and sacred places/ Throughout the hidden lands/ Are sealed by order, and must be respected/ The one who unhesitatingly takes his place/ Like son succeeding father/ In this land I have blessed as a place of accomplishment/ Will in future/ Meet with me, of that there is no doubt.'

From Gödem's 'Seven amulet box' name inventory of seven hidden lands: 'To the north of the Asura cave at Yanglesho, is the snow peak of Gényen Leru/ Like a victory banner flying high, and on it's south side/ The lotus grove hidden land/ Where a variety of fruits and other products of the earth's bounty grow/ A variety of grains will grow there if cultivated/ There are four gates/ Seven thousand settlements/ Just by going there, one will advance up to the ninth

Bhumi of 'excellent intelligence'/ Performing the protection rite for a piece of land 4 Dom (8 metres) in extent will suffice.'

Those are quotations from the prophetic guidebooks. Then there is Domarpa Mingyur Dorjé's song of realisation: 'This place, naturally attracting the common and supreme (Siddhi-s)/ Is the Khechari realm of lotus light/ Only Yogi-s with Karmic destiny/ No others will be able to reach it/ Or even if they reach, they will feel disenchanted/ And wish to return to their homes/ Like the example of the moth and the candle flame.'

Kyapjé Chatral Sangyé Dorjé's song of praise to the Yolmo sanctuary: 'I, Sangyé Dorjé, the joyful mendicant/ Planted the banner of attainment in this sacred place/ And was rewarded with the attainments due in this life.'

And in his 'Evocation of the hidden valley': 'First and foremost, Buddha Padmasambhava/ Set foot in and blessed/ The Yangdak Chok meditation cave in the upper valley/ The self-arisen sun and moon cave in the lower valley, and so on/ Even now, the meditation caves and self-manifest images/ Of the Mahaguru and his consort/ Are directly visible/ The father Guru's kindness is beyond imagining/ As is known to all who have come after him....

From now on, sermons, empowerments and the like/ All superficialities that go under the name of service to living beings/ To discard them, and in this hidden valley/ Engage continuously, day and night, in the practice of the luminous Great Perfection, that is my prayer....

Father Padma saw that future generations/ Would need (the hidden valley) in a time like this, and set it aside for them/ People of little fortune, even myself, have actually reached it/ To get to stay here, what happiness!/ To leave one's corpse behind here, what a joy!'

The Yangdak Chok Meditation Cave, Heart of the Sanctuary

As already quoted from the 'Crucial inventory': 'In the northern hills resembling a precious Stupa/ Is a cave facing southeast/ That is the sacred place where I, Padmasambhava of Odiyana, performed meditation on Yangdak Chok/ From the peak above, one can see the (Asura) cave at Yangleshö/ Those who go there will be freed from birth in the lower realms/ I declare that those who meditate on devotion to me, Padmasambhava/ Shall see my face and/ Attain the Siddhi-s of the supreme Mahamudra in this life', so it was praised in the undeceiving Vajra prophecy of the Mahaguru of Odiyana.

According to the 'Variegated jewel garland' Nepal itinerary by Shamar Chöki Wangchuk: 'At the sacred meditation retreat of Yangdak Chok, the rear mountain is covered with a mixture of forest, meadow and glacial scree, as if enclosing all by design, and the mountain in front is like the overlapping folds of a gown. Among all the lands of India and Nepal, it has the clear form of a natural Mandala. The mountain ridge to the right, like a five-pronged Vajra, encloses the site like an ornamental drape. In the centre is a rocky hill piled up like a heap of wish-fulfilling jewels, and at it's centre is a cave of attainment, broad and imposing. There is a rock overhang like a canopy of the gods. Happy and at ease, the mind becomes clear. Consciousness is relaxed, and there is an upsurge of joy. Above the cave, on a broad and even boulder, footprints of the Dakini-s are quite clear, and there is a Parikrama path of the Dakini-s. Inside the cave is the Guru's headprint, a self-manifest effigy of the Guru, and so on. Extraordinary blessing, treasure of the ocean of wonders beyond compare. In the meditation caves of princess (Mandarava) and (Yeshé) Tso-gyel are many forms, wondrous self-manifest secret Bhaga, the footprints of the eight Dakini-s and five prophesied capable ones. To preserve the Guru's footprint, Mandarava covered it with a rock, and on the cracked surface of a large composite rock nearby are amazing images of treasure containers, amulet boxes and so on, once genuine sources of treasure. Later, the four Dakini-s were seen playing there, but disappeared when (people) came near, and one can see there the gaming boards on which they played. In the rock is one resembling an Indian style gaming board, and in one way of seeing, there are many forms of triangular matrices, and what are said to be the self-arisen volumes of the teachings of the nine vehicles, a nine-level square playing board on the surface of the rock, and so on. There are many such things. In any case, simply going there clarifies one's consciousness, it is an exceptional holy place which transforms perception.'

In Trinlé Düjom's 'Passing the long days of spring' autobiography: 'Ema! This great sanctuary, this hidden valley/ Blessed by the Guru/ Gathering place of the Matrika-s and Dakini-s/ At this meditation cave of Yangdak Chok/ The rear mountain of glacial scree and meadow is splendid and beautiful/ The fore mountain is in the form of crossed hands/ The mountains to either side are like adorning drapes/ A succession of excellent configurations, lovely to behold/ At the centre of a remarkable scree slope/ Like a cascade of jewels/ Is the self-arisen cave of brilliance/ To see it is to open the door to Samadhi/ Occupying it, the mind is at ease/ Intelligence becomes sharp and consciousness clear/ Non-conceptual Samadhi arises in one's awareness/ A blessing of incomparable quality/ In the environs are a great many amazing signs and seals/ Supreme assembly hall of the Daka-s and Dakini-s/ Definitely produced spontaneously/ Overhead are massive white clouds/ The sides of the valley wreathed in mist and vapour/ Softly falls the rain of Siddhi-s/ Happy, peaceful solitude/ Ground covered with lotus flowers/ Surrounded by fragrant trees/ Where many exceptional medicinal incense (plants) grow/ The sweet sound of divine birdcall/ All beings who see, hear, recall or touch/ Such a wonderful holy place as this/ Close the door to rebirth in the lower realms/ So it was said by the Guru himself/ Thus, all beings from the highest to the lowest/ Should strive fiercely with their three doors/ To visit this supreme and special holy place and honour it with clouds of offerings/ Having gained undivided faith/ In this hidden valley/ And especially this place of attainment/ I thus recall the attributes of the place to mind.'

On the identification of the four borders of Yolmo, the 'Crucial inventory' says: 'In between Mangyul to the west/ And Nyanang to the east, it's upper reaches closed by snow/ And lower reaches closed by forest/ There is a protected valley....

(Among) these three valleys is/ The Yolmo snow enclosure/ In between Mangyul and Nyanang to the south....'

The 'Guide to the hidden valley of Padma Tsal' says 'It's configuration is as follows/ Summit overlooking the meeting of six uplands/ The joining of three valleys/ At the throat of the high snows/ To the north of Vajrasana/ Northeast of the city of Li/ At the foot of the land of Mangyul/ At the throat of the Buddha's own devotee/ At the throat of the western side of the chief of the twelve territorial goddesses ....

It starts from the Dagam Namgo (sanctuary) of the north....'

This should be identified as the Langtang bordering the foot of Mangyul, since the hidden land of Dakam Namgo was identified with Langtang by Rikdzin Domarpa Mingyur Dorjé, following the guide to holy places by Tértön Tseten Gyeltsen. From the upper valley in the north to the lower valley in the south should be reckoned a four day journey. The 'Essential inventory of Yolmo' says: 'The valley known as the Yolmo snow enclosure/ At the foot of Mangyul/ Northeast of the city of Li/ South of the snow mountain like a firmly planted victory banner/ West of the Yaksha snow queen/ There are three major valleys/ And three minor ones/ A journey of four days from top to bottom....'

The upper valley in the north must be identified with the snows on the border between Yolmo and Tibet. The 'Essential guide' says: 'The mountains of the upper valley are all snow covered', and the 'Essential inventory': 'The upper valley is blocked by snows....thus is it known as the enclosure of snows.'

The lower or southern reach these days is generally identified with Melamchi Pul, which I suppose is correct. From the 'Essential inventory': 'The Yolmo snow enclosure, hidden valley of the south, and root of all sacred places/ On the lower side, towards India and Nepal, are six minor valleys resembling the fingers of a Yaksha/ Ascending the middle of them/ Brings one to the meeting of three valleys/ The entrance to that valley is where the commoners and subjects gather.'

Concerning the east, the 'Guide to the hidden valley of Padma Tsal' says only this: 'It starts from the splendid mountain pastures to the east....In the east, it touches Nyanang.'

On the protector spirits of Yolmo, the 'Guide to the hidden valley of Padma Tsal' says: 'In that valley, the wild carnivores that appear should be offered to (Gényen) Leru/ The Yeti-s that appear should be offered to Dorjé Lekpa/ The birds and rodents that appear should be offered to Chati Kang/ By doing so, the seven thousand settlements will go to the Sukhavati paradise.'

The 'Essential Guide' says: 'As that sanctuary is entrusted to the territorial spirits Dorjé Lekpa/ Gényen Leru/ and Chati Lhatsen/ An offering of pure ritual cakes stuck with vulture feathers will give a true prognosis/ Proceed after making offerings to the territorial spirits....

When going there, do so without anger or conflict/ If one's consciousness gets disturbed along the way/ Pray singlemindedly to the Guru/ Reaching there, when various miraculous phenomena, sounds and signs appear/ Make offerings and play music for the local Dakini-s and territorial spirits/ Pray to the Guru....In that holy place, do no harm to wild animals and other beings/ If such things occur, make offerings to Leru, and the aggression of wild carnivores will be pacified/ If offerings are made to Dorjé Lekpa, the aggression of Yeti-s will be pacified/ If offerings are made to Chati, the aggression of birds and rodents will be pacified/ In general, praying to the Guru will pacify suffering, circumstances and obstacles.'

According to the 'Essential exposition' inventory of prophecies for the Yolmo snow enclosure: 'As that valley is entrusted to the territorial spirit Dorjé Lekpa, shrines to him should be established to the southeast/ Religious law should be enforced in that valley by a religious king/ Pollution must be avoided/ Living creatures not harmed/ Bathing and cleanliness observed/ By doing so, the valley will know perfect content.'

The Gényen Leru, Damchen Dorjé Lekpa and Chati Lhatsen directly mentioned in the Guru's prophetic guides, and the Jomo Yangri mentioned in the life stories of Jétsun Mila, Shakya Sangpo and Surya Sengé, these are the guardian spirits of the Yolmo snow enclosure. The actual nature of these protectors is that of wisdom deities, but in the terms of mundane perception, they undertook to protect the hidden lands and the teachings in the presence of Orgyen Chenpo (Guru Padma), and appear in the guise of Gényen (male) and Mentsün (female) territorial spirits.

On the names of this sacred place, the 'Guide to Padma Tsal' says: 'It is also known as the Yolmo snow enclosure/ And the name 'hidden lotus grove' is also there.' The 'Crucial inventory' says: 'In particular, those living in the Tö region (upper Tibet)/ Flee to the snow enclosure of Yolmo!/ On the east side of the Tashi Tséringma snow mountain/ Northeast of the city of Li/ Is the valley known as 'Hidden lotus grove'/ It has the complete form of a standing lotus.'

The biography of Shakya Sangpo in Jamgön Kongtrül's 'Lives of the hundred Tértön-s' records: 'Following prophecies, he proceeded to the hidden lotus grove valley, also known as the Yolmo snow enclosure.' Domarpa Mingyur Dorjé's 'Essence of benefit and joy' identification of Namgo Dagam says: 'For ordinary beings like myself, bereft of clairvoyance, the important fact of the identity of Langtang with Namgo Dagam, and the identity of the 'lotus grove' with Yolmo, was not previously understood', and in Trinlé Düjom's autobiography: 'My birthplace is the land praised by the Buddha Bhagavan/ and the Acharya (Padma), the second Buddha/ It's outer form is the Yolmo snow enclosure in Nepal/ It's inner form is the hidden 'lotus grove' valley/ It's secret form is the self-manifest palace of Heruka, indivisible from the glorious Charitra.'

In Kyapjé Chatral Sangyé Dorjé's 'Evocation of the hidden valley': 'The western hidden land of the Yolmo snow enclosure/ Also known as 'lotus grove'....', and in his song of realisation, 'Praise of the Yolmo sanctuary': 'On the border between Tibet and Nepal/ Is the Yolmo sanctuary, the hidden 'lotus grove'....', and thus it is known as the Yolmo snow enclosure in outer form, the hidden lotus grove in inner form, and the self-manifest palace of the Heruka in secret form.'

Abstaining from harming living creatures in this holy place is of great importance. Generally speaking, for those who take refuge in Buddhism, refraining from harming living creatures is part of the refuge commitment, but in particular, to kill or harm creatures in a hidden valley such as this is not only a grievous sin, but will disturb the protector spirits, and bring about obstacles and inauspicious happenings, so beware. From the 'Essential Guide': 'There is a total prohibition on hunting....In this valley, wild animals and living creatures must not be harmed.' From the 'Essential exposition' inventory of prophecies for the Yolmo snow enclosure: 'Avoid pollution/ Do not harm living creatures/ Observe bathing and cleanliness/ By doing so, this valley will know perfect content.' From the 'Essential inventory': 'In the upper valley, enforce a ban on hunting/ In the lower valley, enforce restricted access/ Enforce religious law and royal law....Because it is under religious law, when worshipping Pashupati and Brahma, do not perform sacrifices or offer flesh and blood!' The 'Guide to Padma Tsal' says: 'To ban hunting will ensure the king's longevity', and in Chatral Rinpoché's 'Evocation of the hidden valley': 'Wild animals roam at ease/ The bad Karma of the butcher and the sin of eating flesh and blood are unknown there even in name.'

In the degenerate age in general, and especially in this sacred place, whatever obstacles and difficulties arise, it is important to pray to the Guru. The 'Essential Guide' says: 'If there is sleet or mist/ Or one cannot find the way/ Pray to the Guru!....If one proceeds while making prayers to me, Padma/ One will travel the path.... When going there, do so without anger or conflict/ If one's consciousness gets disturbed along the way/ Pray singlemindedly to the Guru/ Reaching there, when various miraculous phenomena, sounds and signs appear/ Make offerings and play music for the local Dakini-s and territorial spirits/ Pray to the Guru/ Whatever happens, there is no need to fear or be discouraged/ Maintain the dignity of the meditation deity.... In general, praying to the Guru will pacify suffering, circumstances and obstacles.'

The 'Seven chapter prayer' (to Guru Padma) goes: 'For any faithful and Karmically qualified aspirant/ Who prays to me with fervour/ Due to exceptional Karmic cause and effect, auspicious conjunction and aspiration/ My compassionate response is swifter than that of other Buddha-s/ (Thus) Tso-gyel continually prays with devotion.'

The great one of Odiyana (Guru Padma) declared: 'From any faithful man or woman/ Padmasambhava never departs but sleeps at their door/ I was neither born nor will I die/ For every faithful individual, there is a Padmasambhava.'

Although there are innumerable prayers to Guru Padma, the seven line prayer and the Vajra Guru Mantra are universally known.

I suppose that most of the Yolmo people are, generally speaking, of Tibetan origin. This is quite evident from the fact that whether one considers religion and culture, spoken and written language, customs, song and dance, cuisine, costume etc. they are hard to differentiate. Even the slight differences are accounted for by the colloquial expression 'Every valley has it's own language, every Lama has his own version of religion.'

Thus, ever since many noble upholders of the teachings came to Yolmo intending to reach the Guru's hidden land, and settled there, as we have seen, fŏr the most part it goes without saying that they brought heartfelt devotion to the Lama-s and the Dharma with them. However, there are still quite a few Tamang and lowland people living in lower Yolmo.

In addition, that beginners striving to reach the level of liberation and omniscience must first practice in solitary places accords with the spirit of the scriptures and commentaries. The scriptures say: 'If there are many, they will fall into dispute with each other/ If there are two, they will chat to each other/ Stay alone in tranquility/ Like the bracelet of an (unmarried) girl.'

The Moon Lamp Sutra says: 'Renounce attachment to cities and communities/ Rely constantly on the solitude of the forest/ And before long you will attain the supreme Samadhi.'

In the 'Call to altruism': 'From a place of complication or strife/ It is best to distance oneself by one hundred Yojana-s/ Where there are negative emotions (Klesa)/ Do not remain there even for an instant.'

The Ratnakaranda Sutra says: 'For beginners, to fully pacify their minds and thoroughly subdue themselves, they must remain in solitary places.'

The Sutra requested by Purna: 'Staying in mountains and forests/ Multiplies the production of good qualities/ By relying on such solitary places/ One renounces attachment to the five sense pleasures in their entirety/ In the absence of distractions/ The practice of virtue does not decline/ He who does not frequent others, nor engages in discussion/ Who does not speak/ But pursues the solitude of complete pacification in solitary places/ Is adored by the Buddha-s/ Therefore, the Bodhisattva must continually remain in solitary retreats/ With no longing for the city.'

The Samadhiraja Sutra: 'Compared with one who worships all the Buddha-s with offerings of flowers, incense, food and fine preparations for as long as the aeon endures/ One who merely takes seven steps towards a solitary retreat with the mind of renunciation accumulates a boundless mass of merit of a greater order.'

The 'Collective understanding of all the Buddha-s' Sutra: 'To meditate in such places for a single day/ Brings one nearer to accomplishment than a year of meditation in an ordinary place.'

The Siksasamuccaya: 'One must develop patience to seek out the teachings/ Then stay in the forest/ Strive in meditative equipoise/ Meditating on the ugliness (of worldly existence) and so on.'

The Bodhicaryavatara: 'The animals and birds of the forest/ And the trees, cannot be described as unpleasant/ With such easily befriendable companions/ I would gladly stay/ To a cave, or abandoned temple/ Or beneath a mighty tree/ I would go in an instant, without looking back/ And rid myself of the passions/ Calling no place my own/ But naturally abiding in open spaces/ Enjoying freedom and non-attachment/ There I would gladly stay/ With very few possessions, like an alms bowl/ Wearing cloth rejected by others/ Even if this body is never buried/ May I remain there without fear.'

From the 'Resting in the nature of the mind' by the omniscient Longchenpa: 'For as long as the mind does not gain stability/ And is completely deluded by external objects/ One should remain in the solitude of the forest.'

Jétsun Milarepa said: 'Fearing death, I went to the mountains/ And, meditating on the uncertain time of death/ I reached the real stronghold of immortality/ Eschewing all fear of death.'

This brief history of Yolmo was composed at the encouragement of the bilingual Punya Prasad Parajuli and Padam Singh Gale , these two, in view of it's importance not only to tourists but to all pilgrims, and as Tibetan readers are few, Punya Parajuli undertook to translate it into Nepali. At the repeated requests of many others too, I, Khenpo Nyima Dondrup, did so, with an emphasis on easy comprehension, and without recourse to any formal structure. I have summarised the prophetic guides to Yolmo, and my earlier 'Jewel Mirror' history of Yolmo, supplemented with a few other sources.
Boudhanath
May 3rd 2009
or
the tenth day of the 3rd month of the Earth Ox year
the 2,553rd year since Buddhanirvana

With this account of the historical narratives of the Yolmo snow enclosure, king of hidden lands, I confess any transgressions, irrelevancies or errors before the ocean of the three refuges and the three roots. May the source of benefit and joy, the Jina-s' teachings, grow and flourish! May the upholders of the teachings live long! May all mother sentient beings be liberated from cyclic existence and attain unsurpassed and perfect awakening!

English translation by Matthew Akester
Boudhanath, December 2009

The whole of Yolmo is a valley hidden by Guru Padma, but here I briefly list just the Guru's meditation caves, places mentioned in the guidebooks, and the seats of the historic masters:

1. The Yangdak Chok meditation cave
the meditation cave of the Guru and his consorts, and meditation place of the saints of the past, the innermost heart of the sanctuary

2. Chhu Yenlak Gyéden – water with the eight good properties
this is the 'glacial stream of water with the eight qualities' on the upper slopes mentioned in the 'Essential inventory'. It is above Jématang.

3. Jémathang (Bemthang) – sand plain
the place where Kyapjé Chatral Rinpoché actually saw a four-storey tall figure of Dorjé Drolö

4. Marku Tsho – lake of clarified butter
the lake where Damchen Dorjé Lekpa tempered the steel for the Guru's Purba daggers and so forth

5. Tongshong cave
a cave of the Guru re-opened by Kyapjé Chatral Rinpoché

6. Yangri Gang
the temple of the prophecies on the Yangri mountain, protectress of the sanctuary, where Gödem's disciple Drupchen Palden Gyeltsen, Drupthop Gyeltsen Bum, Rikdzin Surya Sengé and Trinlé Düjom all founded temples.

7. Chhati Gang
a mountain, the abode of the protector Chhati Lhatsen.

8. Tshokar Tshonak – black and white lakes (Gosainkunda)
In the 'Unmistaken jewel mirror' guide of Drakar Chöki Wangchuk, it says: 'The 'outsider' Vedic tradition regards (these lakes) as a sacred place of Mahesvara and Uma, while the 'insider' Buddhists regard it as the palace of Cakrasmavara, but for Rikdzin Jé, it was the palace of the goddess Remati, to the north-east of Vajrasana.'

9. Yolmo Nortsho – the lake of Yolmo's wealth
above Tshokar Tshonak, to the east

10. The Nyinda Rangjön meditation cave - ('with a naturally formed sun and moon symbol')
cave of the Guru and his consorts in Melamchi, mentioned in Kyapjé Chatral Rinpoché's 'Evocation of the hidden valley'.

11. Khandro Sangphuk
the secret cave of the Dakini-s (Milamchi Gyang)

12. The Amitabha temple at Milimchhim (Milamchi Gyang)
the seat of Zilnön Wangyé Dorjé

13. The Guru's jewel millstone
as mentioned in the 'Guide to Padma Tsel'. It is preserved in the Amitabha temple.

14. Orgyen Pésha – the Guru's lotus hat
the print left by the Guru's hat, near Tarkado

15. Nakoté
a monastery of the Changtér tradition.

16. The self-manifest stone Stupa
near Lhégang

Guide to the Hidden Land of the Yolmo Snow Enclosure

17. Néding
meditation place praised by Kyapjé Chatral Rinpoché as a second Tsari
(the holy mountain in southern Tibet)

18. Self-manifest conch (image)
near Néding

19. Tsuti Gön monastery
the seat of Shakya Sangpo's successive incarnations

20. Drupné Pema Chöling – 'lotus Dharma sanctuary'
the monastery of Langra Gyalsa, seat of Térwön Nyima Sengé and
Trinlé Düjom.

21. Drupé Drong – 'meditators' village'
hermitage originally offered to Surya Sengé by local people, and later
occupied by Gen Rikdzin Rinpoché, Chatral Rinpoché and so on.

22. Götsang Ling – the 'vulture's nest sanctuary'
originally a residence of Götsangpa, then the seat of Karma Chösang
and his descendants, and latterly a monastery of the 'Rainbow'
tradition.

23. Lhakhang
monastery of the 'Rainbow' tradition, and meditation hut of Chatral
Rinpoché

24. Yolmo Bhakhang Tashi Ghyatsho Monastery
monastery founded by the previous incarnation of Drukpa Rinpoché.

25. Takphuk Sengé Dzong – Lion fort tiger cave
the meditation place of Jétsun Milarepa. there was a monastery of the
'Rainbow' tradition, and at present the nun's retreat centre established
by Khenchen Tsultrim Gyatso.

26. Gang Yul
monastery of the 'Rainbow' tradition, monastery of the Drukpa Kagyu
order, and a Gélukpa nunnery. According to Shamar Rinpoché's guide,

this is the place mentioned in the prophetic guidebook: 'The centre is like a jewel-filled platter/ The king's abode should be established there....'

27. Shingkun Ché – a Stupa in the 'descent from heaven' style containing the remains and relics of Humla Rinpoché Kunga Dorjé

28. Chhumik – spring
a monastery of the 'Rainbow' tradition

29. Near Chhumik, according to Khamtrül Jigmé Trinlé, marks left by the Guru's Purba dagger when liberating Naga-s and demons, and the hoofprint of Ling Gésar's horse

30. Sermathang – plain of gold
a monastery of the 'Rainbow' tradition, and a meditation hut of Chatral Rinpoché.

31. Kazhe
a monastery of the Changtér tradition.

32. Peltsok
According to Shamar Rinpoché's guide, this is the place described in the prophetic guide: 'To the south is a mountainside of forest and meadow/ At it's centre, build a temple of Avalokitesvara and/ A domain for all....' There is a monastery of the Changtér tradition.

33. Tunbu
according to Shamar, the place to make cake offering rituals to the Guru. These days it is known as Timbu.

In addition, there are other monasteries of the family and teaching lineages of the above mentioned Lama-s, belonging to the Changtér and 'Rainbow' traditions, and newly built monasteries and hermitages which are not mentioned in this guide, but it does cover most of the amazing natural holy places throughout the upper, lower and middle parts of Yolmo.

Pilgrimage Route Map of Beyul Yolmo Gangra

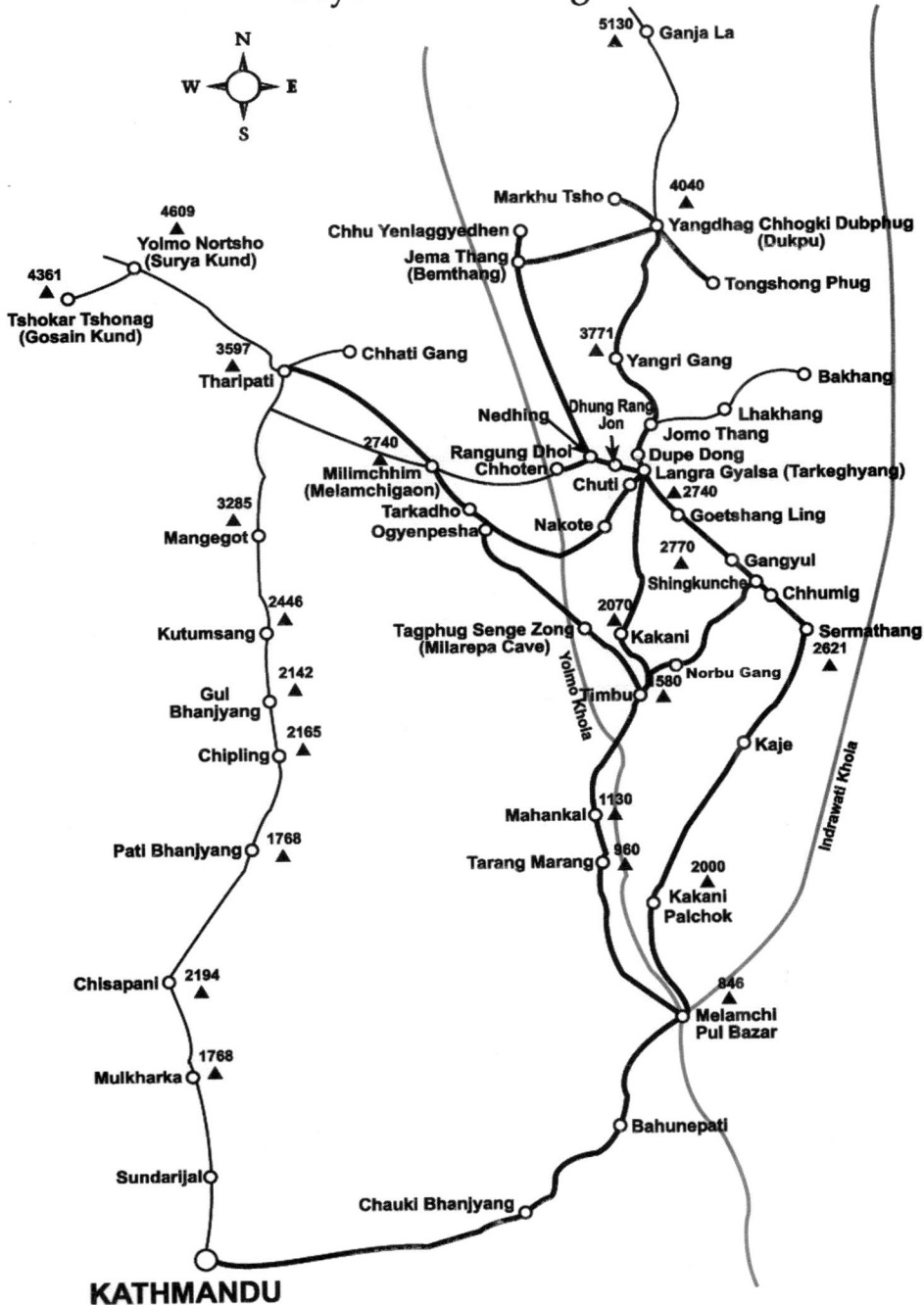

N
W E
S

5130 ▲ Ganja La

4609 ▲
Yolmo Nortsho
(Surya Kund)

4361 ▲
Tshokar Tshonag
(Gosain Kund)

Markhu Tsho

4040 ▲ Yangdhag Chhogki Dubphug
(Dukpu)

Chhu Yenlaggyedhen

Jema Thang
(Bemthang)

Tongshong Phug

3597 ▲
Tharipati

Chhati Gang

3771 ▲

Yangri Gang

Bakhang

Nedhing

Dhung Rang
Jon

Lhakhang

Jomo Thang

2740 ▲
Milimchhim
(Melamchigaon)

Rangung Dhoi
Chhoten

Dupe Dong

Langra Gyalsa (Tarkeghyang)

Chuti

2740 ▲

3285 ▲
Mangegot

Tarkadho
Ogyenpesha

Nakote

Goetshang Ling

2770 ▲

Gangyul

Shingkunche

Chhumig

2446 ▲
Kutumsang

Tagphug Senge Zong
(Milarepa Cave)

2070 ▲
Kakani

Sermathang
2621 ▲

2142 ▲
Gul
Bhanjyang

Norbu Gang

Yolmo Khola

Timbu

580 ▲

2165 ▲
Chipling

Kaje

Indrawati Khola

1130 ▲
Mahankal

1768 ▲
Pati Bhanjyang

Tarang Marang

960 ▲

2000 ▲
Kakani
Palchok

2194 ▲
Chisapani

846 ▲
Melamchi
Pul Bazar

1768 ▲
Mulkharka

Bahunepati

Sundarijal

Chauki Bhanjyang

KATHMANDU

1. HH Penor Rinpoché at Nangkyi Gang on his visit to Yolmo

2. HH Jadral Rinpoché and HH Dodrup Rinpoché at Néding

3. Jadral Rinpoché at Néding

4. The Yangdak Chok Cave

5. Chhu Yenlak Gyéden

6. Jémathang (Bemthang)

7. Marku Tsho

8. View of the Tongshong Phuk Cave

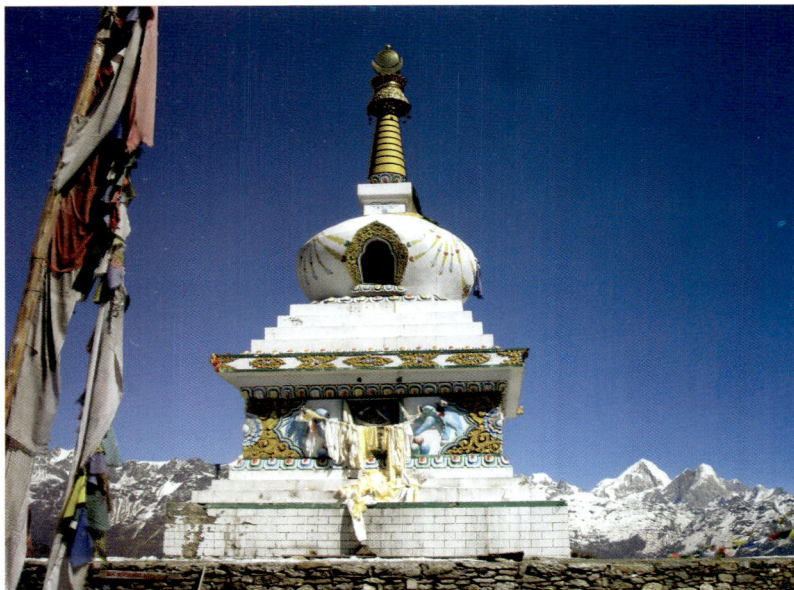

9. Newly built Stupa at Yangri Gang

10. Dorjé Lekpa

11. Tshokar Tshonak – Black and White Lakes (Gosainkund)

12. Chhati Gang

13. The Nyinda Rangjön Meditation Cave (at Melamchi Gyang)

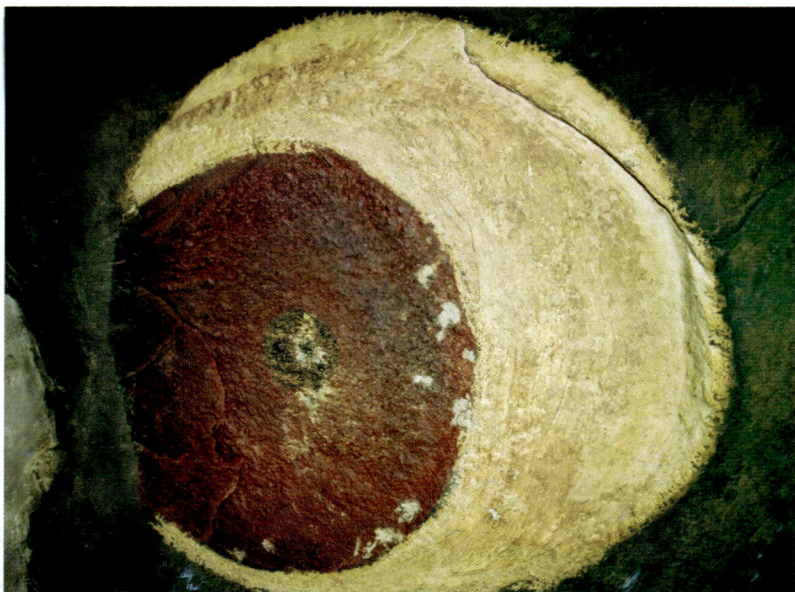

14. The Nyinda Rangjön

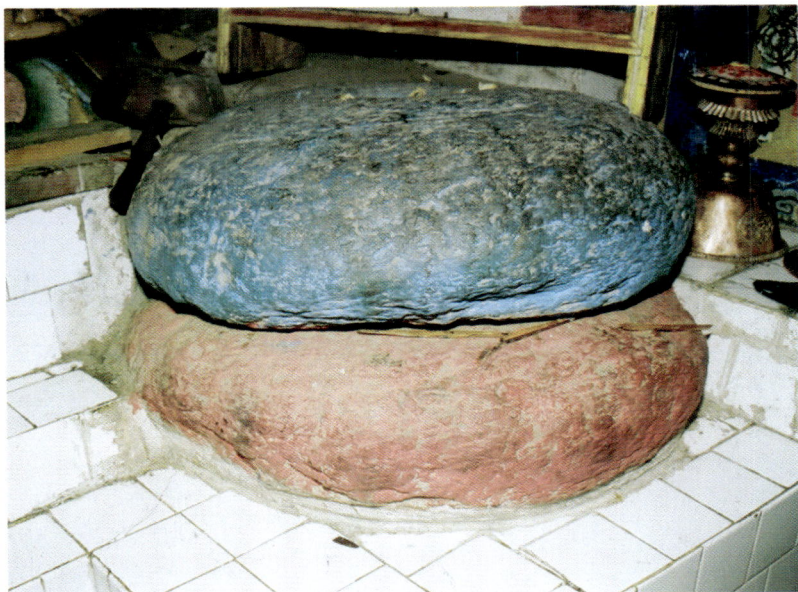

15. *The Guru's Jewel Millstone*

16. *Khandro Sangphuk (Milamchi Gyang)*

17. Milimchhim (Melamchi Gyang)

18. Orgyen Pésha

19. The self-manifest stone Stupa (near Lhégang)

20. Néding

21. Self-manifest conch (near Néding)

22. Tsuti Gön

23. Nakoté

24. View of Drupé Drong, Langra Gyalsa, Dhenthang etc.

25. Langra Gyalsa (Tarké Gyang)

26. Takphuk Sengé Dzong

27. Götshang Ling

28. Gang Yul

29. Near Chhumik, marks left by the Guru's Purba dagger

30. Stupa at Shingkunche

31. Chhumik

32. Sérmathang

33. Lhakhang

34. Yolmo Bhakhang Tashi Ghyatsho Monastery

35. *New statue of Guru Padmasambhava (at Palri Pema Odsal Chhoeling)*

36. *Kazhe*

37. Palchok and Kakani

38. Tunbu (Timbu)

39. View of Yolmo Gangra (Yolmo valley) from Nagarkot